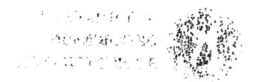

# What Will the Weather Be Like Today?

*Pour la famille Bony*
P.R.

To my mother
From Kazuko

Also illustrated by Kazuko
*Cuckoobush Farm*

Also by Paul Rogers
*From Me to You*

**Acknowledgments**
*What Will the Weather Be Like Today?* Text copyright © 1989 by Paul Rogers. Illustrations copyright © 1989 by Kazuko. First published in the United States by Greenwillow Books. Reprinted by arrangement with Greenwillow Books, a division of William Morrow & Company Inc.

Photography
**33** (lightning) (sky) images Copyright © 2000 PhotoDisc, Inc.  **33** (snow) Lori Adamski Peek/Tony Stone Images  **33** (girl) Michael Keller/FPG International  **34** (l) Bob Torrez/Tony Stone Images  **34** (tr) Scott Barrow/International Stock  **34** (br) Jeremy Walker/Tony Stone Images  **35** (tl) Sunstar/International Stock  **35** (m) John Warden/Tony Stone Images  **35** (tr) Artville  **36** Stock Image/Zephyr Images  **36** (br) Tom Pantages  **37** Timothy Shonnard/Tony Stone Images  **37** (br) Joel Benjaman  **38** (t) Timothy Shonnard/Tony Stone Images  **38** (bl) Nicole Katano/Tony Stone Images  **38** (br) Lori Adamski Peek/Tony Stone Images  **33–38** (borders) images Copyright © 2000 PhotoDisc, Inc.

Houghton Mifflin Edition, 2005

PRINTED IN CHINA
ISBN: 978-0-618-03645-5
ISBN: 0-618-03645-8
18 19-DBS-08 07 06

# What Will the Weather Be Like Today?

## PAUL ROGERS
## PICTURES BY KAZUKO

 HOUGHTON MIFFLIN     BOSTON • MORRIS PLAINS, NJ

California   •   Colorado   •   Georgia   •   Illinois   •   New Jersey   •   Texas

# Just at the moment
# when night becomes day,

when the stars in the sky
begin fading away,

you can hear all the birds
and the animals say,

"What will the weather be like today?"

5

# Will it be warm?

# Will there be snow?

Or a frost?

Or a storm?

"Be dry," says the lizard, "and *I* won't complain."

The frog in the bog says,
"Perhaps it will rain."

The white cockatoo
likes it steamy and hot.

The mole doesn't know
if it's raining or not.

"Whatever the weather,
I work," says the bee.

"Wet," says the duck,
"is the weather for me."

"Weather? What's that?"

say the fish in the sea.

The world has awakened.
The day has begun,

and somewhere it's cloudy,

and somewhere there's sun,

and somewhere the sun
and the rain meet to play,

and paint a bright rainbow
to dress up the day!

# How is the weather where *you* are today?

# Checking the Weather

# What is the weather like today?
# How can we find out?

Is it hot or cold today?
How hot or cold is it?
A thermometer will show us.

Is it windy today?

How windy is it?

A wind gauge will show us.

Is it rainy today?

How rainy is it?

A rain gauge will show us.

# How else can we find out?
# We can go outside and see!